The Blessed Life of Christian Singles

By Reverend Joseph Saunders

Edited, Designed, and Published by:

Desktop Prepress Services
Donna L. Ferrier
808 S. New Bethel Blvd.
Ada, OK 74820
1-866-220-4160
http://www.desktopprepress.com

Printed in the United States of America.

ISBN 978-0-6151-5679-8

Table of Contents

Introduction

Your Singleness is A Blessing

oday, many Christian singles all over the world are needlessly living out their lives in mental torment. They want to be married, and they want to be married right now! And the older singles get, the worse this mentality becomes. They start taking God's will into their own hands. They start dating non-believers, or travel great distances across the country (or even across the world) on some wild goose chase for their mate thinking that God wants them to do so. And the advent of the internet has opened up the entire world for desperate single Christians to look for their mates. But guess what? God does not want us to live out our lives in desperation!

This book will provide a Bible-based perspective on many issues facing single Christians today, such as:

- Singleness
- Marriage
- Divorce and remarriage
- Masturbation
- Loneliness
- Premarital sex

As the author, I will also discuss my own walk with God as a single Christian to provide a "like-minded" example for other Christians. Mind you, not all Christians are like-minded. Some are carnal; some are lazy. But whatever our spiritual state, we are all in the same body of Christ, but we are to love one another.

The most important point to remember throughout this book is that God wants us to be fulfilled, and the only person who can provide true fulfillment is Jesus Christ. Jesus is perfect; people are imperfect. If we cannot trust Jesus in the perfect person of God to fulfill our needs, how can we possibly expect an imperfect person to accomplish that task?

To God be the glory if you want to get married because marriage is a gift from God. But so is your singleness! Don't let anyone tell you any different. If your church pushes you to the back of the pews because you're single, declare your freedom in Christ, declare that your life is a blessing, and by all means find another church to attend!

In 1 Corinthians 7, the Apostle Paul thoroughly describes single as well as married life, and I advise all single Christians to read that chapter, particularly if you've never done so. But in the first verse he says, "It is good for a man not to marry." A little further down in verses 32-35, he says:

"I would like you to be free from concern. An unmarried man is concerned about the Lord's affairs---how he can please the Lord. But a married man is concerned about the affairs of this world-how he can please his wife---and his interests are divided. An unmarried woman or virgin is concerned about the Lord's affairs: Her aim is to be devoted to the Lord in both body and spirit. But a married woman is concerned about the affairs of this world---how she can please her husband. I am saying this for your own good, not to restrict you, but that you may live in a right way in undivided devotion to the Lord."

Paul's concern for the Corinthians in this passage was that they live however they can best serve the Lord. Singles can do more for the Lord because they don't have the concerns of a spouse to worry about. And at some point in your life, God may call you to be married, but as long as you're single, Paul makes it clear that you can do more for the Kingdom of God at this stage of your life than you'll be able to do when you're married. Serving the Lord is a gift, not a curse! If you find that you're consumed with worry about getting married, focusing on the Lord's service will take your concentration off yourself and put it where it belongs---on Him! Serving the Lord is what should consume us.

Some singles are called to be single for life, although some Christians operate out of misguided notion that no one is called to be single because Genesis 2:18 says, "It is good for the man not to be alone." But note how God says, "the man," and not "a man," or "all men." Remember, one word can change an entire context of what a verse says. Verse 24 says, "For this reason a man will leave his father and mother and be united to his wife, and they will become one flesh." Notice again how God says, "a man," and not "all men."

It's also important to remember that Jesus never married, and since Jesus came to fulfill the Law, if marriage was a requirement of that Law, He would have had to get married. Instead, He was the perfect single minister, and our perfect role model for how to live our lives as single Christians today. Jesus was always ministering wherever He went; so should we be as well.

In addition, Matthew 19:10 makes it clear that while not everyone is called to singleness, those who can accept the calling should do so. Beginning in Matthew 19:4-9, Jesus comments on the permanence of marriage and says that anyone who divorces his wife except for marital unfaithfulness commits adultery. Afterward, in verse 10, His disciples said to Jesus, "If this is the situation between a husband and wife, it is better not to marry." Next, in verses 11-12, Jesus makes it clear that those who can accept a calling to be single should do so:

"Jesus replied, 'Not everyone can accept this word, but only those to whom it has been given. For some are eunuchs because they were born that way; others were made that way by men; and others have renounced marriage because of the kingdom of heaven. The one who can accept this should accept it.'"

The bottom line is: If singleness is your calling, great! If being married is your calling, great! But whatever your calling is, your life are a blessing, and anything you can do for the Lord, great or small, is a blessing.

Chapter 1

Fearfully and
Wonderfully Made

healthy spiritual mindset starts with a healthy perspective on who Jesus created us to be. I used to teach at the Equally Yoked Christian singles ministry in Falls Church, Virginia, and I covered many topics with numerous singles. One day I spoke on the topic, "What Is An Ugly Person?" Many times, in our search for a soulmate, we become ruled far too much not only by what a prospective partner looks like, but what we look like as well. As a result, we strive to be perfect on the outside, all the while neglecting our spiritual insides, which is the most important part of us. While looks may be very important to you, they're not very important to the Lord.

According to Genesis 1:26-27, and Genesis 9:6, we were created in God's own image. In Genesis 1:31, God saw all that He made, and said it was good. That includes you and me because we are part of God's creation. In fact, we're the most special part of His creation because He created nothing else in Him image except us. I realize that now, we all have a fallen nature, but Jesus came to save the lost, and if we are walking in the light of Christ, then we are still good because He is good. And our current bodies will be resurrected back to life one day, just as Jesus was. So, if you're a Christian and someone calls you "ugly," that person obviously doesn't realize he or she is talking to a body that will be glorified in heaven one day according to 1 Thessalonians 4:15-17. Verse 17 in particular speaks of our eternal blessings with Christ:

"Then we which are alive and remain shall be caught up together with them in the clouds, to meet the Lord in the air: and so shall we ever be with the Lord."

So, the question becomes, "Do you despise God's creation?" We despise God's creation every time we think of ourselves or another person as ugly. The truth is every one of us was fearfully and wonderfully made. If you don't believe me, read Psalm 139:13-14:

"For you created my inmost being; you knit me together in my mother's womb. I praise you because I am fearfully and wonderfully made; your works are wonderful, I know that full well."

Notice in that Psalm that David says he knows full well the Lord's works are wonderful. Do you know full well that you are a wonderful creation of the great I AM? Do you dare think of yourself as ugly? Are you going to be the one to tell the Lord that in all of His perfection, He made a mistake in how He created you? Are you going to tell Him He made a mistake in how He created someone else? If you do, you discredit His creation. And we have all done this at some point in our lives---whether we're kids on the playground gawking at the "fat kid," or whether we're in the office envying someone else's looks or physique. God has already given us "all spiritual blessings" in Christ Jesus, according to Ephesians 1:3-6. It's up to us whether we want to fully experience those blessings, but we can't do it while we're caught in the sin of discrediting the creation of the great I AM. Ephesians 1:3-6 says:

"Praise be to the God and Father of our Lord Jesus Christ, who has blessed us in the heavenly realms with every spiritual blessing in Christ. For he chose us in him before the creation of the world to be holy and blameless in his sight. In love he predestined us to be adopted as his sons through Jesus Christ, in accordance with his pleasure and will-to the praise of his glorious grace, which he has freely given us in the One he loves."

Notice that this scripture says we were chosen by God before all creation to be holy and blameless. Do you realize what an honor that is? Do you realize how special that one thought makes you? You will understand once you're transformed by the renewing of your minds (Romans 12:2), which produces enlightenment. Do not be like unbelievers, for they are blind to all things God, according to 2 Corinthians 4:4:

"The god of this age has blinded the minds of unbelievers, so that they cannot see the light of the gospel of the glory of Christ, who is the image of God."

Instead we need to have the mind of Christ, portrayed in 1 Corinthians 2:15-16:

"The spiritual man makes judgments about all things, but he himself is not subject to any man's judgment: 'For who has known the mind of the Lord that he may instruct him?' But we have the mind of Christ."

Bottom line: the unbeliever does not understand the things of Christ; the spiritual man can make spiritual judgments. Which do you want to be?

Let's look at Leah for a moment in Genesis 29. Leah was one of the wives of Jacob and the oldest sister of Rachel. According to verses 17-18, Leah was the less desirable of the two because she had weak eyes, while Rachel was beautiful in form. She was so beautiful that according to verse 19, Jacob was willing to work seven years for her father, Laban, in order to get her. At the end of the seven years, however, Laban decided to deceive Jacob and give him Leah instead. But even though Jacob's plan didn't work the way HE wanted, Leah produced four children, including two that spawned the Israelite tribes Levi and Judah. Levi was the tribe responsible for serving the Lord in the temple full time. Judah is the tribe that our Lord and Savior Jesus Christ came from. Even though Rachel was blessed as well, Leah gave birth to two of the most important tribes of all time! So, my single friends, do not look at the outside of a person; instead, look at how God is manifesting His plan in that person's life.

Brother Boaz in the book of Ruth understood this very well. For even though in Ruth 2:5, Boaz notices Ruth from afar, according to verses 11-12, Ruth's spirit caught his attention even more. He says:

"I've been told all about what you have done for your mother-in-law since the death of your husband---how you left your father and mother and your homeland and came to live with a people you did not know before. May the LORD repay you for what you have done. May you be richly rewarded by the LORD, the God of

Israel, under whose wings you have come to take refuge."

And the Lord, God of Israel, did indeed reward Ruth. For the blessed union between she and Boaz produced Obed, who was the father of Jesse, who was the father of King David, whose lineage spawned our Lord and Savior. God is ready to bless you, too, just like He blessed Leah and Ruth. Are you ready to trust in Him? 1 Corinthians 2:9-10 says:

"However, as it is written, 'No eye has seen, no ear has heard, no mind has conceived what God has prepared for those who love him' but God has revealed it to us by his Spirit. The Spirit searches all things, even the deep things of God."

And Romans 13:15 says: "May the God of hope fill you with all joy and peace as you trust in him, so that you may overflow with hope by the power of the Holy Spirit."

These are promises of God for those who truly love Him. Notice that the 1 Corinthians passage says the Spirit searches the deep things of God, not the flesh. Even though I don't know what God has planned for your life, He does, but the only way you're going to find out is if you ask Him. We have not because we ask not according to James 4:2. But Psalm 37:4 says, "Delight yourself in the LORD and he will give you the desires of your heart."

The bottom line is that Jesus didn't rise from the grave on the third day just for who we would consider the "pretty people" to be. In fact, Scripture shows us time and time again the truth of 1 Corinthians 1:26-28:

"Brothers, think of what you were when you were called. Not many of you were wise by human standards; not many were influential; not many were of noble birth. But God chose the foolish things of the world to shame the wise; God chose the weak things of the world to shame the strong. He chose the lowly things of this world and the despised things---and the things that are not---to nullify the things that are…"

When outside appearance outweighs the spiritual inside appearance, we tread on dangerous ground. We should be enjoying every moment of our Christian singleness, and not live in a state of mental and spiritual bondage. For when we are in bondage, we cannot worship the Lord the way He wants us to, and we cannot experience the full blessings that God has for us as singles. In fact, many of us miss God's blessings because we worry too much about where we want to be in the future, instead of concentrating on performing the tasks for the kingdom that He has created for us to do right now. When we think too far ahead, we lack the capacity to minister to those in the here and now because we lose our spiritual focus. Thinking about the future is not a sin, but worrying about it is. Do not let worry rule you to the point that it detracts from your ministry here and now. Be patient. Trust in the Lord with all your heart and lean not on your own understanding (Proverbs 3:5-6). If you do, He promises to direct your path.

And do not blame your current situation on the devil just because you're unhappy. Jesus gave us victory over sin, but unfortunately, many of us are living like we're still in bondage to it. Attributing our lives to Satan is the ultimate dishonor toward God because God did not make a mistake in having us where we are. And Satan most certainly did not put us where we are. So trust that God will bring your desires to pass. Life in the Spirit brings the abundance of God's overflowing love for us.

Finally, keep in mind that people watch and listen to everything we say and do as believers. When we live in mental torment, people see that. So, why should the lost want to be saved, if the saved people are living in just as much torment as the lost? Matthew 5:17 commands us, "In the same way, let your light shine before men, that they may see your good deeds and praise your Father in heaven."

Being a spirit-filled Christian is fun, but if you are not walking in the ways of Christ, then you will miss your blessings. So, while you're single, get involved in the work of the Lord! Find a good singles ministry, and be yoked with like-minded singles. Get to know God's will for you life. Have fun, just because God wants you to. Live like the free person you already are (whether you know it or not) because of your faith in Christ Jesus! There are so many things you can be doing right now for the kingdom of God. And in doing them, God may very well introduce you to the person He wants you to be with. Free yourself from the bondage of your flesh and renew yourself in the Spirit of God.

Chapter 2

"Should I Even Get Married?"

If you're single and believe that God has called you to be married, it helps to know what biblical marriage entails and what singleness entails, so that you can know for sure whether you truly desire to get married or remain single. Let's start by examining 1 Corinthians 7 once again, beginning in verses 32-35:

"I would like you to be free from concern. An unmarried man is concerned about the Lord's affairs---how he can please the Lord. But a married man is concerned about the affairs of this world-how he can please his wife-and his interests are divided. An unmarried woman or virgin is concerned about the Lord's affairs: Her aim is to be devoted to the Lord in both body and spirit. But a married woman is concerned about the affairs of this world-how she can please her husband. I am saying this for your own good, not to restrict you, but that you may live in a right way in undivided devotion to the Lord."

The first century Christians of Paul's day were being persecuted heavily, and Paul was trying to save them from their troubles. He wasn't saying that singleness has no troubles of its own. Rather, he was being a good watchful apostle trying to save his people from as much trouble as he possibly could. And one thing he acknowledges is that married couples have more concerns than single people because, as the passage says, the married man is concerned with how to please his wife, and the wife is concerned with how to please her husband. Singles have no such concerns, and are therefore free to devote more time to the Lord.

As far as concerns for married couples, one concern is sexual immorality, which is one thing Paul was trying to save married couples from in his day. Verse 2 says that Paul gave these instructions about marriage because of all the immorality in the world at the time. That's why he said in verses 2-5:

"But since there is so much immorality, each man should have his own wife, and each woman her own husband. The husband should fulfill his marital duty to his wife, and likewise the wife to her husband. The wife's body does not belong to her alone but also to her husband. In the same way, the husband's body does not belong to him alone but also to his wife. Do not deprive each other except by mutual consent and for a time, so that you may devote yourselves to prayer. Then come together again so that Satan will not tempt you because of your lack of self-control."

In these instructions, he wanted to make sure that the marital commitment would not be broken because of temptation. This same concern exists heavily among Christian married couples today. And even today, married people still have more concerns than single people, singles still have more time to devote to the Lord, and Christians worldwide are still being persecuted. So, these scriptures are just as applicable now as they were in Paul's day. In the end, he says in verse 6-7:

"I wish that all men were as I am. But each man has his own gift from God; one has this gift, another has that."

Here you can see that Paul prefers his singleness to that of getting married, but he also acknowledges that the Lord gave people different gifts, and different callings, which are to be used to glorify the Lord. Here again, he also wanted to save his people from the pain and trouble that is associated with married life and wants them to focus completely on serving the Lord as he is able to do.

If you desire to marry, however, God will make that happen. If you've ever seen the Lord lead two people together, instead of Christians trying to force relationships on their own, it's a beautiful thing. Everyone around the couple automatically knows through the Holy Spirit that God has drawn them together for success in their upcoming married life. A lot of confirmation happens when Jesus leads two people together. And know this as well: the person Jesus picks for you many times won't be the person you would choose for yourself.

One reason singles try to force the issue of marriage is because they burn in lust. Paul says in verses 8-9:

"Now to the unmarried and the widows I say: It is good for them to stay unmarried, as I am. But if they cannot control themselves, they should marry, for it is better to marry than to burn with passion."

This is not a license to pull someone off the street and head straight for the altar just because you can't control your passions. That would make us no better than animals acting on a mating instinct. Remember, God created us in His image, so that give us special distinction, and it's important to understand your position in Christ as a Christian single. Other scriptures in the Bible still apply, such as not being unequally yoked with nonbelievers (2 Corinthians 6:14), trusting the Lord to direct your path (Proverbs 3:5-6), and leading an active prayer life as Jesus did throughout His ministry. James 4:2 also says that we have not because we ask not. So, if your desire is to be married, commit that to the Lord in prayer regularly. And while you're waiting patiently for an answer (and this does not mean waiting in mental and spiritual torment), make sure you maintain an active connection to God through prayer, scripture reading, and ministry work. If you're living a sedentary, idle Christian life, then you will be living life in defeat and in the lusts of the world, and that includes sexual lust. God always want to bless us, but many singles have not put themselves in a position to receive those blessings.

And while you're doing God's work, one day, God will place that special person in your life, and you will know it. But remember, even when that happens, true fulfillment only comes from Christ. A spouse is never intended as a replacement for God. There are so many unhappy married people who wish they were single. So, remember, marriage is not the answer to fulfillment, so don't look to your spouse to replace God in fulfilling your life. He or she will not be able to do that. If marriage was the answer to fulfillment, the divorce rate in this country (and in the church) wouldn't be nearly as high as it is now. Marriage is about two people seeking the Lord together, not putting one another on Christ's throne.

That is why if we chose to marry, we need to be complete in

Christ beforehand. Positionally, we are complete in Christ, but we need know that in our hearts. Contrary to the world's (and even the church's) perception, we are not "half people" until we get married. How many times have you heard someone in church say, "God chose John to complete Sue"? God didn't create us as half people walking around waiting for our other half to complete us. He created us as complete people from the beginning, and we need to realize that before we step onto the altar of marriage. All we need for completion is Jesus Christ; marriage is extra.

Some of the most effective Christians in the Bible were single, including Jesus Himself. And scripture does not mention any of the apostles or John the Baptist as having wives, except Peter. His mother-in-law is referenced in Luke 4:37-39. Now, some, like Dan Brown, will argue that Jesus had a wife. This is a false claim. If Jesus had been married, it would have slowed down His mission. Jesus was always on the move, and that tone is carried heavily in the book of Mark in particular.

I like to call Paul the second greatest single of all time, the greatest being Jesus, as previously stated. Without a doubt, Paul led his single Christian life under the guidance of the Holy Spirit, which means that all of contributions to the New Testament were Spirit-directed as well. 2 Timothy 3:16 says that all scripture is God-inspired, which means that Paul's instructions were inspired by God as well.

Singleness keeps us active as well, just like Jesus and Paul. When two people get married, they tend to relax, let their hair down, and "let themselves go." It's as if they just ran a race, crossed the finish line, and stopped to be sedentary from that point on. But what they don't realize is that married people have to keep themselves up to the same standard that attracted them to their spouses to begin with. It takes very hard work, true dedication, and commitment.

It's understandable that once you have the person of your dreams, you'll want to relax and "call it a day," but in reality, that kind of attitude is not going to work in most cases. When people find their soulmates, they want the same candle that lit their candle to burn forever in marital love. Relaxing often gets couples in trouble because circumstances don't always change for the better.

I'm saying this because if you do decide to marry, you'll want to take heed of which pitfalls to avoid. And if you want to get married, you should be preparing yourself for marital success while you're single, and knowing which pitfalls to avoid beforehand will help you do that. So don't relax to the point that it leads to marital distress.

In reality, the "relax" mode leads to marital distress that is really a thirst for being complete in Christ. I pray that singles and couples alike can only completely relax in Christ Jesus. For He says in Matthew 11:28-30:

"Come unto me, all ye that labour and are heavy laden, and I will give you rest. Take my yoke upon you, and learn of me; for I am meek and lowly in heart: and ye shall find rest unto your souls. For my yoke is easy, and my burden is light."

This message is nothing new; it's the same message that many of you heard as children. It's the same message the apostles heard as children, and the same message the reformer Martin Luther heard as a child as well. Ecclesiastes 1:9 says "there is no new thing under the sun." But many of us cannot move to the next level in our spiritual growth because we have not learned at the level where we currently are. God wants to honor and bless you today. Are you in position to receive His blessings?

Chapter 3

Seeking After The Spirit

n May 2003, I attended the National Singles Retreat at The Cove in Asheville, North Carolina, which offered different workshops, as most singles retreats do. Scanning the written program, the workshop entitled, "My Flesh Runneth Over" caught my eye because I can definitely relate to the concept being relayed in that title. In fact, I think most Christian singles can relate to their flesh running over. The workshop was heavily attended by both men and women. Upon our arrival, the presenter gave each of us a "pop quiz," where we had to write down at least three characteristics we desired in a mate. When we were finished, we discovered that more than 80 percent of the class desired fleshly characteristics, and only 20 percent desired spiritual traits. What a travesty!

Christian singles always need to be seeking after the things of the Spirit of God, as indicated in Colossians 3:1-2, and that applies in our dating relationships: "Since, then, you have been raised with Christ, set your hearts on things above, where Christ is seated at the right hand of God. Set your minds on things above, not on earthly things."

At no time does Scripture encourage anyone to seek after fleshly desires. In fact 1 Corinthians 6:11-13 speaks of fleshly desires as a person's past life when that person has been spiritually reborn through Jesus Christ: "And that is what some of you were. But you were washed, you were sanctified, you were justified in the name of the Lord Jesus Christ and by the Spirit of our God." Verses 12 and 13 go on to say that we can seek after all the fleshly desires we want, but this is not a beneficial approach to living out our daily lives:

"Everything is permissible for me---but not everything is beneficial. Everything is permissible for me---but I will not be mastered by anything. Food for the stomach and the stomach for food-but God will destroy them both. The body is not meant for sexual immorality, but for the Lord, and the Lord for the body."

The point of this passage is that fleshly desires are temporary and unsatisfying. When applied to the single life, men look for an attractive slender woman who is a sharp dresser, well-educated and cooks. Women look for a tough, well-built man, who is financially stable, owns his own home, and drives the best car. But to whom are those desires beneficial? Yourself or God? Beauty deteriorates with age. Most people gain weight after marriage. People who exercise vigorously during their single life very often don't have time after they start a family. A person can lose a home or a job in a day. The question remains: If your "ideal" person lost his or her economic status and good looks, would you still love that person? What's left to love if you're only seeking to fulfill fleshly desires? This is why single Christians must be seeking after the things above as evidence of our transformed lives in Christ Jesus, as indicated by Colossians 3:1-3:

"Since, then, you have been raised with Christ, set your hearts on things above, where Christ is seated at the right hand of God. Set your minds on things above, not on earthly things. For you died, and your life is now hidden with Christ in God."

One other point that is very timely and worthy of comment is that unfortunately, we are living in an age where more and more Christians are choosing to make fornication (sex outside of marriage) a part of their dating lives, and more and more people are choosing to live together rather than get married. Christians, be warned! 1 Corinthians 6:9-10 say that such people will not inherit the Kingdom of God! Notice in this passage, fornicators are lumped together with drunkards, idolaters, and adulterers, to name a few:

"Know ye not that the unrighteous shall not inherit the kingdom of God? Be not deceived: neither fornicators, nor idolaters, nor adulterers, nor effeminate, nor abusers of themselves with mankind, Nor thieves, nor covetous, nor drunkards, nor revilers, nor extortioners, shall inherit the kingdom of God."

In addition, Revelation 21:8 indicates that the sexually immoral will meet the same end with murderers and occult followers:

"But as for the cowardly, the untrustworthy, the vile, the murderers, the sexually immoral, those who misuse drugs in connection with the occult, idol-worshippers, and all liars---their destiny is the lake burning with fire and sulphur, the second death."

Many times throughout my Christian walk, I sought things that led to mental, emotional, and spiritual destruction. This left me confused, frustrated, and always in a state of "want," until I made up my mind and heart that my life was only going to be led by Jesus Christ, and not desires of the flesh that "looked good," but left me unsatisfied in the end. What a difference it made in my life when I started seeking after the things of the Spirit!

When you seek after the things of the Spirit of Christ, God will take you to new spiritual heights and reward you abundantly. You will receive fresh revelation and be a great blessing to others. But before we can be a blessing to others, we have to bless God. How can we accomplish this? By exercising our faith, which comes directly from the leading of the Holy Spirit. According to Hebrews 11:6, "And without faith it is impossible to please God, because anyone who comes to him must believe that he exists and that he rewards those who earnestly seek him."

Note that this scripture says that God rewards us when our faith pleases Him. Since Jesus bought us with a price according to 1 Corinthians 6:20, God is pleased when we do right by Him. Ask yourself, "Am I doing right by God right now?" Romans 12:2 says that in order to do right by God, our minds have to be transformed:

"And be not conformed to this world: but be ye transformed by the renewing of your mind, that ye may prove what is that good, and acceptable, and perfect, will of God."

Notice that this scripture says the transformation of our minds is necessary to discovering what God's perfect will is. The problem in the lives of many single Christians is that their minds are not being transformed and renewed so that they desire the things of God. Not being transformed, however, can cause stagnation in our walks with Him. Romans 8:12-14 warns of the consequences of living according to the flesh:

"Therefore, brethren, we are debtors, not to the flesh, to live after the flesh. For if ye live after the flesh, ye shall die: but if ye through the Spirit do mortify the deeds of the body, ye shall live. For as many as are led by the Spirit of God, they are the sons of God."

In addition, Paul urges the Christians in Ephesians 4:25-32 to put off any unwholesomeness or falsehoods, which manifest themselves in the flesh:

"Therefore each of you must put off falsehood and speak truthfully to his neighbor, for we are all members of one body. In your anger do not sin. Do not let the sun go down while you are still angry, and do not give the devil a foothold. He who has been stealing must steal no longer, but must work, doing something useful with his own hands, that he may have something to share with those in need. Do not let any unwholesome talk come out of your mouths, but only what is helpful for building others up according to their needs, that it may benefit those who listen. And do not grieve the Holy Spirit of God, with whom you were sealed for the day of redemption. Get rid of all bitterness, rage and anger, brawling and slander, along with every form of malice. Be kind and compassionate to one another, forgiving each other, just as in Christ God forgave you."

Not putting off fleshly lusts will hinder our growth and even cause death according to the Romans 8 passage. So, how do you know that your growth is being hindered? If you're not seeing the blessings that you desire, then it's time to reexamine your walk. It's possible that God could be testing you to see if you will remain faithful even if He doesn't show you the blessings when YOU want them! Or, it could be that you have not "put off" your old self and put on the new, according to Romans 6:6, Ephesians 4:22, Colossians 3:9, and Titus 2:2. So, examine where you are with God now and determine what you need to do to get where you want to be!

Chapter 4

"I'm Called To Be Married"

k. You've read the scriptures on singleness and marriage, prayed over them, listened to Jesus to discern what you believe He wants for your life, and you've decided that you were called to be married, rather than single. Congratulations! Even though Paul said in 1 Corinthians 7 that it's good to be single, GOD IS HAPPY when people get married (or remarried, as we will discuss in the divorce chapter).

A huge problem in our churches today is that singles are not being taught the biblical characteristics of a Godly mate. As a result, they lack spiritual discernment when choosing a mate, so they tend to believe that if someone says he or she is a Christian, it's probably true. Friends, not even close! The fact is, there are many, many, many singles and married couples alike in today's churches, who are not saved or who have stagnant, carnal walks with the Lord. And there are many divorced singles in the church who will tell you, "I thought my spouse was a Christian." So, I feel it necessary to offer up some scriptural points here for what a Godly mate is. We'll start with what Scripture says about marriage from Ephesians 5, and then talk about how this applies to the dating relationship. These marriage scriptures are usually taken way out of context by the church and world alike, so in our discussion, we'll also dispel some of the false doctrine surrounding them.

We'll start with Ephesians 5:22-24, which spells out the order in the marriage household:

"Wives, submit yourselves unto your own husbands, as unto

the Lord. For the husband is the head of the wife, even as Christ is the head of the church: and he is the saviour of the body. Therefore as the church is subject unto Christ, so let the wives be to their own husbands in every thing."

First of all, these scriptures absolutely, positively, DO NOT mean what many people teach---that the husband gives orders and the wife obeys and bows down to him whether she likes it or not. It does not mean that if a husband is beating up his wife, she has to take it in the name of submission. Women have been threatened, beaten, and even murdered by their husbands, and all the while felt they needed to just stay and deal with it because women are supposed to submit to their husbands. This is false doctrine, plain and simple. God's design for marriage is not abuse.

In order to get the entire picture, we have to read the rest of Ephesians 5. The commands for the husband begin with Ephesians 5:25, "Husbands, love your wives, even as Christ also loved the church, and gave himself for it," which describes an incredibly sacrificial love that he is to have for her---the love of Christ. Remember, Christ gave his life for mankind! If you read the rest of that chapter, the rest of what the husband is supposed to do goes from 5:26-29, which compares the love husbands are to have for their wives with the love that Christ has for the church:

"That he might sanctify and cleanse it with the washing of water by the word, That he might present it to himself a glorious church, not having spot, or wrinkle, or any such thing; but that it should be holy and without blemish. So ought men to love their wives as their own bodies. He that loveth his wife loveth himself. For no man ever yet hated his own flesh; but nourisheth and cherisheth it, even as the Lord the church: For we are members of his body, of his flesh, and of his bones."

Ephesians 5 ends with verse 33 saying, "Nevertheless let every one of you in particular so love his wife even as himself; and the wife see the she reverence her husband."

In actuality, the husband has a far more difficult role in the relationship than the wife does because he is supposed to provide Godly leadership for His family to follow. He is commanded to love his wife with the sacrificial love of Christ and providing a Christ-like example for her to follow, and to love her as he loves himself. The marriage is a partnership, not only because the two people are seen as one flesh by God, as shown in Genesis 2:24, but also because if he's not loving her with the love of Christ as the scriptures indicate, then neither she nor the rest of his family has any Godly leadership to follow. If he's providing the leadership he's supposed to be providing, then a woman's husband is someone that she would want to reverence, and not someone she feels she has to.

Think of it this way. Wouldn't you like to be married to someone with the same Godly characteristics you've seen in close friends or family members? The fact is, if your boyfriend or girlfriend is not growing in Christ, if he or she is not growing into a Godly man or woman, then that person is not a good marriage prospect at that point in his or her life. Men, how are you treating your girlfriends? Are you nurturing them spiritually? Are you drawing them to Jesus? Are you providing that sacrificial, Christlike example? Ladies, are your boyfriends drawing you closer to Jesus? Do you respect him? Do you have spiritual conversations? Do you pray together? And are you both continuing to grow in Christ as individuals as well as a couple? Any woman who is dating someone she knows she won't be able to respect and follow into a marriage partnership needs to get out of the relationship. God is a God of purpose, not in doing something just for the sake of doing it. Dating for dating's sake is a worldly concept.

In addition, feminism has crept into our singles groups. Some women believe that it's ok for them to ask men out and take the lead in the dating relationship. They usually believe this because 1) they don't have a dating partner and want one so bad that they're willing to sacrifice God to get what they want or 2) their boyfriends aren't the Godly men they should be in and of themselves. But if the woman is the one taking the lead in the relationship, how is he supposed to be prepared to be a family leader if the relationship progresses to the point where the two of them get married? Don't look for something miraculous to happen on the altar after you both say "I do." As with any other major life decision, God has His timing for our lives. God is not sexist, and has specific roles for each of us, and those roles are spelled out in scripture.

Christians need serious spiritual discernment in the area of dating, and we need to be praying for growth in this area. Not every-one who says he or she is a Christian is. 2 Corinthians 6:14 says:

"Be ye not unequally yoked together with unbelievers: for what fellowship hath righteousness with unrighteousness? and what communion hath light with darkness?"

"Missionary dating," or dating a nonbeliever in hopes the other person will get saved, is out of the will of God according to the above verse because as soon as a Christian starts dating a nonbe-liever, for whatever reason, he or she is already going against God. And there are some really "good, moral heathens" in the world, but these people cannot encourage you in Jesus. As soon as you get past the superficial conversations and start talking about spiritual matters, the two of you will part ways faster than Moses parted the Red Sea. "Almost saved" doesn't even count in horseshoes. If your dating partner is not saved, he or she cannot even begin to follow Paul's teachings in Ephesians 5 if the two of you should get mar-ried because Paul was speaking to believers. An unsaved man or woman can't love someone with the love of Christ, because he or she has no idea what that means since it has never manifested in his or her own life.

Again, congratulations on your decision to get married in God's perfect timing. If you keep looking to God, praying, study-ing His Word, and serving Him during your time as a single per-son, in His time (not yours), He will bring alongside you the Godly person He wants you to spend your life with. And if the two of you are looking to the Lord in your own personal walks, as well as together as a couple, you will be able to serve Him together in your marriage covenant. Remember, there are three of you in that covenant---Jesus, you, and your mate.

Chapter 5

"I'm Divorced; Can I Remarry?"

s an ordained Baptist minister, I see the repercussions divorce has on singles because I have to counsel singles who used to be married. Divorced singles generally have many more issues to cope with than never-married singles because circumstances surrounding divorce can be extenuating and traumatic. If you've been hurt by divorce but have decided to remarry, I say go for it, as long as it's the will of God. Even though 1 Corinthians 7:1 says it's good for a man not to marry, 1 Corinthians 7:2 says that because of all the immorality in the world, each man should have his own wife, and each woman should have her own husband. 1 Corinthians 7:8-9 also says it's better to marry than to burn with passion.

Unfortunately, so many people in the church try to tell people who have been married that it's wrong for them to remarry and use the book of Matthew to try to make their point. The Pharisees were in error from the beginning of their talk with Jesus because they were trying to test Him. In Matthew 19:3, the Pharisees ask Jesus, "Is it lawful for a man to divorce his wife for any and every reason?" Clearly their hearts were not right with Jesus and they had no answer for their own question. Jesus responded in verses 4-6 with:

"Haven't you read," he replied, "that at the beginning the Creator 'made them male and female,' and said, 'For this reason a man will leave his father and mother and be united to his wife, and the two will become one flesh'? So they are no longer two, but one.

Therefore what God has joined together, let man not separate."

Verse 7 indicates that in the Old Testament, Moses permitted a certificate of divorce, but this was not always true from the beginning. According to Matthew 19:8, Moses only permitted divorce because the people's hearts were hardened. God's design in the in the Garden was that the two become one flesh, and this is echoed in Matthew 19:5-6:

"'For this reason a man will leave his father and mother and be united to his wife, and the two will become one flesh'" So they are no longer two, but one. Therefore what God has joined together, let man not separate."

Even though it's not cool to divorce, things happen in a marriage, and divorce is a reality. But the good news is that we are all saved by the grace of God. Many divorced singles feel inadequate to minister in the body of Christ because they feel condemned by the church, and because many of them had been married for years and simply don't know how to function as single people. Remember, though, there is no condemnation for those who love the Lord. So, if you belong to Christ, there is no condemnation in you. God can use anything. He used the betrayal of a close friend to save the world. If He can do that, He can use divorced singles to accomplish His will.

So many churches tell people that if they've been divorced, they can never remarry. I beg to differ, however. Divorce is sad, yes, but God is faithful. Many people, for example, never knew the Lord before they went through a divorce, so God used that experience to draw them to Him. As a result, they may marry someone else in Christ, and God may show them what marriage was really designed to be because that person's heart is right with God, and there is no condemnation for those who are in Christ Jesus, according to Romans 8:1. So, yes, those people can remarry and still be in the will of God.

And remember that all sin equals death, according to Romans 6:23. And singles who have never been married have committed plenty of sins, just like anyone else. No one should be pointing condemning fingers at divorced singles. God hasn't condemned them if they love the Lord, so, what right do we have to condemn them? The second half of Romans 6:23 is that the gift of God is eternal life in Jesus Christ our Lord. Christ came so that we could be free!

Unfortunately, a lot of Christian divorced singles are not living free because of some strange doctrine that's not in the Bible, or because the body of believers is shunning them. But marriage comes from God. It was God's design way back in the Garden of Eden in Genesis 2:23-25:

"And Adam said, This is now bone of my bones, and flesh of my flesh: she shall be called Woman, because she was taken out of Man. Therefore shall a man leave his father and his mother, and shall cleave unto his wife: and they shall be one flesh. And they were both naked, the man and his wife, and were not ashamed."

Marriage makes God happy. If you remarry GOD IS HAPPY!

One thing I do advise. Before God throws a party in heaven because you and your boyfriend, girlfriend, or fiancé have decided to get married, make sure that person is in the will of God. And make sure you've worked out any issues from your previous marriage before entering into the next one. So many divorced singles jump right back into marriage because it's the only life they've ever known, and they don't know how to function as single adults. The problem is that many times they've never dealt with the consequences of their previous marriage. As a result, they end up dragging unnecessary baggage into their next marriage and make life harder on themselves. Make sure that you learned from your last marriage so you can experience the greater blessings of God and move forward with Jesus leading the way. What's past is past. Go to premarital counseling, and also ask people who have been down the same road that you are getting ready to go down about remarrying. If you do not have any friends who have been remarried, then pray and ask God to send someone in your path to guide you. If you truly believe in your heart, that God will send someone, it will come to pass because it is the promise of God, according to Proverbs 3:5-6:

"Trust in the LORD with all thine heart; and lean not unto thine own understanding. In all thy ways acknowledge him, and he shall direct thy paths."

Ask your pastor, a trusted church member, or another Christian to help you and pray for you. Find someone who has the spirit of the Lord as Paul did in 1 Corinthians 7:40. There is so much help available, but we have to do our part and ask for it. So, divorce single, there is still hope.

GO FOR IT!

Chapter 6

"Do I Have To Be Celibate Until I Get Married?"

eeping your virginity until you are married is not only a very Godly thing to do, but it will also save you from a lot of heartache and pain that come with losing your virginity. When you give yourself to someone before you are married, you have not only cheated yourself from the blessings that come from keeping your virginity, but you have also cheated on God. Whether you are male or female, God looks at His church like a bride. If you belong to Jesus, you belong to his church. So we, the church, are the bride of Christ.

Many Christian singles have had premarital sex at some point in their lives, and as a result, feel like they "blew it." They feel they cannot be the very best in Christ because of their past. Having premarital sex even one time produces horrible emotional and spiritual baggage. It's true that people who have premarital sex and don't have Jesus in their lives have no hope, but for those of us who have Jesus in our lives, we can praise God and shout "Glory Hallelujah!" for what He did on the cross because it means that we have hope! So, even if you've had premarital sex, you can still "measure up" to be the very best in Christ. "How?" you may ask. "I gave myself up before I married," you say. Acts 10:33-35 says:

"Then Peter opened his mouth, and said, Of a truth I perceive that God is no respecter of persons: But in every nation he that feareth him, and worketh righteousness, is accepted with him."

Wow! This is great news! You know we often hear the first part of this verse, that God is no "respecter of persons," but we don't seem to hear the second part as much---that God works His righteousness into anyone who fears Him. It doesn't say that righteousness depends on how much or how little we've sinned. For Romans 3:23 says, "For all have sinned and fall short of the glory of God." Romans doesn't say that only those who have had premarital sex fall short of the glory of God. It says "all" have sinned.

So, if you gave yourself to someone in your singleness, Jesus is here to tell you that He forgives you, and that He can use you anytime, just as you are. Because when it comes right down to it, the only thing any of us can bring to Christ is ourselves, with only His blood giving us the right to do so. That's what the best-loved hymn "Just As I Am," which Christians have been singing since 1835, is all about. Do yourself a favor. Break out a hymnbook, or look up the lyrics on the internet, and sing those words right now. Sing them to the Lord. Doesn't matter what kind of voice you have.

And remember, Jesus died for all of your sins, not just some. Scripture is clear about the cost of sin. Romans 6:23 says:

"For the wages of sin is death, but the gift of God is eternal life in Christ Jesus our Lord."

This scripture proves beyond the shadow of a doubt that Jesus saved us from death. We are all sinners, according to Romans 3:23, and according to this verse, the cost is death. But Jesus gave us eternal life, which saves us from the death we all deserve, no matter what we have or haven't done. Yes, it is true that even when we do repent, we still have to reap what we sow. A woman who gets pregnant as a single person, for example, still has a baby on the way. That's not because God is angry with her. Children are a gift from God. And even though she sinned, when she repents, God forgives her. And as that new mom looks to Jesus, He will guide her in how to raise that child according to His Word.

Samson was a man from God. He knew God and depended on Him at times. But Samson had a weakness---he lusted after women. Now, there's nothing wrong with men looking at women as long as we're not lusting while we're doing it. But Samson viewed women to the point that he fell into sin and took his focus off the mission that God gave him to set his people free. What's worse is that the Philistines knew that Samson lusted after women and used Delilah as a ploy to get him to reveal the secret of his great strength. But even after, the Philistines captured Samson and gouged out his eyes, Samson prayed to the Lord in Judges 16:28 for the Lord to give him his strength back. And as the Lord gave him his strength, the rest of that chapter records that he steadied himself between two pillars and pushed until the entire temple came down on the Philistines. And unfortunately, Samson died with them, proving that Romans 6:23 was true hundreds of years before it was ever written. Samson paid the price for his sin (the wages of sin is death), but when he prayed to God, He still enabled Samson to accomplish his purpose for Israel and completed the work that He wanted Samson to do in the first place.

The bottom line is that God chooses to use us. He doesn't have to. And it's a privilege and an honor to serve Him. The question is, do you want to serve God? Don't let sin drag you down. Confess it, be forgiven, claim that forgiveness, and go forth in power! Sometimes as Christian singles, we get off track and lose our focus on what God wants us to do, but that doesn't mean we're doomed for life. That's not the message of Christ! If you are willing, God can use you, just like He did Samson. God's plan will still be done on earth as it is in heaven. Romans 1:5-6 says:

"because of your partnership in the gospel from the first day until now, being confident of this, that he who began a good work in you will carry it on to completion until the day of Christ Jesus."

He will finish the work He started in you. Doesn't matter which sins you have or have not committed. God still can use you and loves you the same. His love is unchanging.

So, do not feel like you cannot be used because of some past sin that was already forgiven. We are the bride of Christ! Christ sees His bride as a virgin, untouched and unblemished. If you have taken Christ as Lord and Savior over your life, and repented of your sins, then you belong to Christ, and are part of His church, His perfect and unblemished bride. 1 John 1:9 says, "If we confess our sins, he is faithful and just to forgive us our sins, and to cleanse us from all unrighteousness."

The bottom line is that whether you've given yourself to another or not, true abstinence can only be found in Christ. What good does it do a Christian who practices abstinence and ends up sinning against God anyway because that person feels that he or she is more holy than the one who did not remain celibate? How will that profit the Christian who did not keep him- or herself? Paul says in Philippians 1:22, "If I am to go on living in the body, this will mean fruitful labor for me."

So, to the ones who kept themselves, I say to you: Do not let the sins of pride and arrogance arise out of your celibacy. If you've allowed yourself to become prideful, confess it to Jesus, and be forgiven. We're all saved by the same God under the same grace.

The book of Hosea has always been especially inspirational to me because I have not always been faithful to God, but He still uses me despite my shortcomings. Hosea is all about Israel's spiritual adultery; God's unfaithful wife. The book is a prophetic work, and if you read the account, you'll see that when Israel returns to God, He will receive her back in His faithful, full love---the same kind of love God has for His people today when we come back to Him. No matter how messy you feel, Jesus will clean you up if you let Him. Jesus died on the cross for all of our sins, so ask him to forgive you from all wrong doing.

It's also important to know that we should not test God by sinning willfully just because we know we can be forgiven. Hebrews 10:26-27 warns Christians about this:

"If we deliberately keep on sinning after we have received the knowledge of the truth, no sacrifice for sins is left, but only a fearful expectation of judgment and of raging fire that will consume the enemies of God."

Willfully sinning against God brings on a fearful expectation of raging fire and judgment. Jesus wants us to have peace. Philippians 4:7-9 says:

"And the peace of God, which passeth all understanding, shall keep your hearts and minds through Christ Jesus. Finally, brethren, whatsoever things are true, whatsoever things are honest, whatsoever things are just, whatsoever things are pure, whatsoever things are lovely, whatsoever things are of good report; if there be any virtue, and if there be any praise, think on these things. Those things, which ye have both learned, and received, and heard, and seen in me, do: and the God of peace shall be with you."

Today is a new day, and you are a new creation in Christ. 2 Corinthians 5:17 says, "Therefore if any man be in Christ, he is a new creature: old things are passed away; behold, all things are become new." Go forth and celebrate in Christ from this point on.

Chapter 7

"Is Masturbation Ok?"

ingles and couples alike are constantly debating about whether it's ok to masturbate. To answer this question, we need to examine what masturbation is, the motivation behind it, and the desires it produces. Masturbation can be simply stated as self-gratification from sexual emotions. Romans 2:8 warns against the dangers of being self-seeking: "But for those who are self-seeking and who reject the truth and follow evil, there will be wrath and anger."

And 1 Corinthians 6:17-20 says:

"But he who unites himself with the Lord is one with him in spirit. Flee from sexual immorality. All other sins a man commits are outside his body, but he who sins sexually sins against his own body. Do you not know that your body is a temple of the Holy Spirit, who is in you, whom you have received from God? You are not your own; you were bought at a price. Therefore honor God with your body."

Masturbation is actually a form of sexual immorality, so it is by nature, sin. We dishonor our bodies when we engage in this act. Most people don't realize this, but masturbation is more than physical stimulation, because it often begins with something we see or hear that triggers sinful thoughts. We're bombarded every day with sexual images via TV, the internet, magazines, radio, and music. It's everywhere! And it's so easy for those sexual elements to get into our spirit.

We're also bombarded through conversations with other people, which is why we need to be careful of the company we keep. 1

Corinthians 15:33 says, "Do not be misled: "Bad company corrupts good character." Just as Jesus says in 1 Corinthians 6:14-16 that those who unite with prostitutes become one flesh with them, by this same token, we become "one flesh" in mind and spirit with people we talk to. And if non-believers lead us astray because they see things differently than we do and corrupt our way of thinking by their mindset, then we're no better than they are even if we're Christians. James 4:4 says:

"Ye adulterers and adulteresses, know ye not that the friendship of the world is enmity with God? whosoever therefore will be a friend of the world is the enemy of God."

Being friends with the world means being in agreement with the world, and the more we walk in the Spirit, we will truly realize that separation in our hearts. When that happens, we find that we no longer have anything in common with people who aren't in like-mindedness with the Lord, so our conversations, or "friendliness" with the world will cease.

After we see or hear something that enters our minds and becomes a thought, we need to decide whether that thought is sinful. Good rule of thumb: If your thoughts violate scripture, they're sinful, which is why we always need to know what the Word of God says. Hebrews 4:12 says, "For the word of God is quick, and powerful, and sharper than any twoedged sword, piercing even to the dividing asunder of soul and spirit, and of the joints and marrow, and is a discerner of the thoughts and intents of the heart." God will use His Word to convict us of impure thoughts and actions. If you're not experiencing God's conviction on your heart, you may not be walking with the Spirit.

Speaking of thoughts, what do you think about when you masturbate? No, you don't have to answer this out loud in a group of your closest Christian friends in your next Bible study. Really think about it nonetheless. Are your thoughts pure? Probably not. Are your thoughts sexual? Probably. Maybe you're lusting after your boyfriend or girlfriend. But Jesus says in Matthew 5:28: "But I tell you that anyone who looks at a woman lustfully has already committed adultery with her in his heart." The same goes for women looking at men, by the way.

As far as scripture references to masturbation, it's alluded to in

Genesis 38. Judah had three sons. His firstborn son, Er, was married to Tamar. But Er was found to be wicked in the eyes of the Lord, so the Lord put him to death, according to verse 7. Afterward, in verse 8, Judah told his second son, Onan, to lie with Tamar to fulfill the obligation to his older brother of producing children. But when he was having intercourse with her, he spilled semen on the ground, and God was displeased. So, God put him to death, too. Unfortunately, the doctrine that has since formed from that account is that we should marry because God is displeased when we waste semen. But we have to put the story in proper context. Onan didn't fulfill his responsibility to produce children. So, God was not only displeased with him for masturbating semen onto the ground, but He was also displeased that he didn't obey the instructions He gave him. For all Onan knew, that may have been the entire reason he was on this earth, and he blew it.

As singles we need to be very careful that we do not let masturbation or any other sin get in our way of missing our sole purpose here on earth. As Onan teaches us, the most important thing is not what we want for our lives, but what God wants. For whatever reason, Onan didn't want to get Tamar pregnant, but God wanted her to produce children. And that decision by Onan cost him his life. When we don't listen to God and carry out His instructions for our lives, we tread on dangerous ground.

Today, God is calling us to focus on Him and put away the desires of the flesh. Ephesians 2:3 says, "All of us also lived among them at one time, gratifying the cravings of our sinful nature and following its desires and thoughts." Notice the past tense here. Once we become believers, we no longer have the desire to gratify the sinful nature. In fact, Galatians 5:16-17 says that we will not be overcome with sinful desires if we walk in the Spirit:

"So I say, live by the Spirit, and you will not gratify the desires of the sinful nature. For the sinful nature desires what is contrary to the Spirit, and the Spirit what is contrary to the sinful nature. They are in conflict with each other, so that you do not do what you want."

And lastly, Galatians 5:24 says, "Those who belong to Christ Jesus have crucified the sinful nature with its passions and desires." So, if we're truly of Christ, and if we're truly walking with the Spirit, we will have crucified our fleshly desires.

In the end, masturbation boils down to a lack of fulfillment in one's life. It's another "fix" that singles think will bring them everlasting satisfaction. But that can only be found in Jesus. You can still be a Christian and be unfulfilled in certain areas of your life. A preacher of mine once said that Christians are like Swiss cheese. The holes in the cheese represent our weak spots, or areas that only Christ can fulfill. Some singles believe, "As long as I can masturbate and not marry, then I'm good." But in reality masturbation is a hole in many Christians' lives that only Christ can fulfill.

If you struggle with this issue, tell God about it. He already knows anyway. He's just waiting for you to come to Him and give Him all of your troubles. Psalm 34:17 says, "The righteous cry, and the LORD heareth, and delivereth them out of all their troubles." If you have to fast in order to get closer to the Lord to solve this issue in your life, then by all means, do so. But do not keep feeding the flesh. You cannot be truly focused on God and doing work for His Kingdom when you're focused on edifying yourself.

God can help you bring masturbation under control, but the question is, do you want His help? Hopefully the answer to that question is "yes" because of the doors it opens up---doors for more focused devotion and service to Him. God loves us and is always ready to forgive us when we ask and restore us into a right relationship with Him. He did send His Son to die for us after all.

Chapter 8

"Can I Have Premarital Sex?"

remarital sex is a huge concern for Christian singles, particularly since we live in an age where cohabitation is becoming the new "dating." But make no mistake; shacking up is unbiblical. Not only that, but it's been proven time and time again that singles who live together before marriage have the highest divorce rate. So, it's obviously not a great way to "try it out to see if it will work." And friends, if something doesn't work even by the world's standards, that's pretty bad!

Premarital sex is fornication, plain and simple, and there are numerous scriptural references to fornication as sin. Matthew 15:18-20, which is echoed in Mark 7:20-22, says:

"But those things which proceed out of the mouth come forth from the heart; and they defile the man. For out of the heart proceed evil thoughts, murders, adulteries, fornications, thefts, false witness, blasphemies: These are the things which defile a man: but to eat with unwashen hands defileth not a man."

In addition, John 8:41 says:

"Ye do the deeds of your father. Then said they to him, We be not born of fornication; we have one Father, even God."

As you can see, fornication is something to be avoided. In fact, John indicates that fornication is not among the deeds of our Father. There are numerous other scriptures as well, too numerous to list in this short book. For your own study, however, here they are: Acts 15:29, 21:25; Romans 1:9; 1 Corinthians 6:13, 6:18, 7:2, 10:8; 2 Corinthians 12:21; Galatians 5:19; Ephesians 5:3; Colossians 3:5; 1

Thessalonians 4:3; Jude 1:7; Revelation 2:14, 2:20-21, 9:21, 14:8, 17:2, 17:4, 18:3, and 19:2. If all these scriptures aren't enough to convince you that fornication is sin, I'll pray that Jesus opens your heart to see the truth.

The idea that some Christians seem to have that it's ok to have sex as long as it's with the person you're going to marry, is not from God! In fact, many, many engaged couples who have been unable to "wait for marriage" have ended their engagements after sex. Case in point, Romans 6:23 says the wages of sin is death, and pre-marital sex kills relationships. People who have had premarital sex even one time struggle for years to overcome the guilt and regret. They spend years in mental torment when they could have experienced God's blessings instead. The good news is that Psalm 103:12 says, "as far as the east is from the west, so far has he removed our transgressions from us." And Romans 8:38-39 says:

"For I am convinced that neither death nor life, neither angels nor demons, neither the present nor the future, nor any powers, neither height nor depth, nor anything else in all creation, will be able to separate us from the love of God that is in Christ Jesus our Lord."

God forgives, and does not remind us anymore. Are you being reminded? By whom? Whoever it is, it isn't God.

So, why do Christians have premarital sex? Because they're tempted and fall by their own evil desires, according to Matthew 13:15, quoted previously. But know this! God wants to deliver you from evil! Matthew 6:13 says, "lead us not into temptation, but deliver us from evil." God delivers us from evil; He does not tempt us into it. James 1:13 says: "Let no man say when he is tempted, I am tempted of God: for God cannot be tempted with evil, neither tempteth he any man."

Some Christians believe that it's ok to live together if you're not having sex. But this only leads to temptation. A great urban minister, Deron Cloud, has a ministry called "Keep It Real." About 10 years ago, his group performed a play called, "Boyfriend and Girlfriend Thang," which demonstrates what happens when boyfriends and girlfriends behave like married couples. Through the play, Rev. Cloud illustrated that Christians can be messed up for years believing a lie. The "boyfriend and girlfriend thang" is nothing more than bondage from the devil, and the person you're with is probably not who God created you to be with. Unfortunately, Christians lose years and years of blessings because of living a lie. I've had many ups and downs in my Christian walk over the past 14 years, and that play has been a blessing to me to this very day. Hosea 4:6 says: "My people are destroyed for lack of knowledge." Many singles today lack knowledge in their walks with God as singles. This is largely because we don't listen. James 1:9 says everyone should be slow to speak and quick to listen. And the fact is, singles make a lot of excuses for doing what they want to do instead of listening to God. This doesn't apply to everyone, as many singles are doing right by God. Those of you who are in a good relationship with the Lord, help those who are struggling, so they can share in God's blessings with you.

I'm not coming down on anyone, but I do want you to know the truth about premarital sex. Teenage boys are brought up believing that it's ok to lie with a woman before marriage, and that it's good for them to sow their "wild oats" while they're young and single. This is one of the greatest lies boys are told. We need to be teaching our children to serve God and not themselves. No one can serve two Gods. Matthew 6:23-25 says, "No man can serve two masters: for either he will hate the one, and love the other; or else he will hold to the one, and despise the other." I realize this scripture is specifically talking about money, but it doesn't matter which god other than the Lord Jesus Christ you are serving. You still can't serve two masters. I urge you to do as Joshua said in Joshua 24:15 after he led the Jews into the Promised Land, "Choose this day whom you will serve." Who are you going to serve today? The god of lust or the true-living, all-wise eternal Father on the throne? If you are a Christian single living with someone, I warn you that the longer you stay in that situation, the harder it will be to come out of it. God is calling you out of it right now. Make it easy on yourself. Do as He says.

One more thing to consider is 1 Corinthians 6:8-10:

"Know ye not that the unrighteous shall not inherit the kingdom of God? Be not deceived: neither fornicators, nor idolaters, nor adulterers, nor effeminate, nor abusers of themselves with mankind, Nor thieves, nor covetous, nor drunkards, nor revilers, nor extortioners, shall inherit the kingdom of God."

Take note! Fornicators will NOT enter the kingdom of heaven. Do you want to go to heaven?

Once again, this is another fulfillment issue. Many people have sex to try and find fulfillment. In fact, a lot of people only find that so-called fulfillment in the act itself and not the one they are having sex with. No matter how strong the temptation may be to have sex, take note of 1 Corinthians 10:13:

"No temptation has seized you except what is common to man. And God is faithful; he will not let you be tempted beyond what you can bear. But when you are tempted, he will also provide a way out so that you can stand up under it."

God wants to give you a way out of the temptation you're facing right now. Are you willing to take it?

Hebrews 3:15 says, "Today, if you hear his voice, do not harden your hearts as you did in the rebellion." Throughout the Old and New Testament, God has spoken in many different ways. Today, He speaks to us through His Son---the key to eternal fulfillment.

Chapter 9

"I'm Lonely!"

oneliness plays a major role in the lives of many Christian singles. Loneliness is a sign that we have not given all we have to the Lord. And when we don't give all we have to God, we leave a void in our lives that only God can fulfill. We get into trouble when we use other things outside of Christ to fill that void. We reap what we sow, and if we allow loneliness to invade our spirit, we embrace it as part as a God-given struggle. To say, "I am lonely," is to say, in effect, that Jesus is not active in your life. Deuteronomy 31:6, which is echoed in Hebrews 13:5, says that the Lord never leaves us nor forsakes us. In spite of scripture, however, many Christians run around thinking that God is not present. Now hear this! God is always present in the lives of believers.

At any rate, Christian singles cannot allow loneliness to rule their lives. Spending time saying, "I am lonely; I am lonely" over and over again in your mind will only serve to plant the seed of loneliness in your thoughts, where it will grow and spread throughout your entire being. And it will remain inside you, eating away at your spirit, until it is uprooted. So, we need to be very careful about how we think of ourselves. Proverbs 23:7 says, "For as he thinketh in his heart, so is he." Matthew 12:34 and Luke 6:45 say, "of the abundance of the heart his mouth speaketh."

Matthew 14 records a story where Peter was walking on water and began to sink because he took his eyes off Jesus. As he was sinking, he cried out for the Lord to save him. Afterward, the Lord asked Peter in Matthew 14:31, "You of little faith," he said, "why did you doubt?" Note that Peter never answered the question. But this is the same question Jesus is asking His church today when we take our eyes off him. When you are feeling lonely, ask yourself, "Did I take my eyes off Jesus?"

Many times we start out in our Christians walks full of faith, but as time goes on, we get stuck somewhere between the shore and the boat. Not to take away from the other apostles, but Peter was the only one recorded as stepping out in faith. He said in Matthew 14:28, "Lord, if it's you," Peter replied, "tell me to come to you on the water." Jesus simply responds with, "Come" in verse 29. And with that, Peter stepped out of the boat. Like Peter, you may have started out on a good, strong walk, only to sink somewhere in the middle. If so, I have good news for you! All you have to do is call out to Jesus, like Peter did, and he will pull you up from the cursed waters of loneliness. You do not need to drown.

According to Matthew 1:23, Jesus' name is also "Immanuel," which means "God with us." Through the ministry of the Holy Spirit, He is with us at all times and forevermore. Paul says in Ephesians 1:13 that we are sealed with the Holy Spirit of promise. God is not only with us on this earth, but He is also with us forever after we die in these present bodies and enter heaven. You are not alone. Pray, fast, and ask God to remove anything that will hinder your walk with Him and keep you from enjoying the blessings He has for you. God will remove those lonely feelings.

Many Christians also believe they can lose their salvation. That is a lie! No wonder these Christians are lonely! One screw-up, and God leaves! This false teaching needs to be addressed. Remember, God said He would NEVER leave us nor forsake us. Never is never! He never says, "I won't leave as long as you don't make any mistakes." Remember Peter denied Jesus three times, and Jesus knew it was going to happen! The night that Jesus was betrayed, He told Peter, "before the rooster crows, you will deny me three times" (Luke 22:34). When that prophecy came true, Peter ran off weeping. When Jesus rose from the dead on the third day, Mark 16:7 records that the angel told the women who came to the tomb to go tell His disciples and Peter that He's risen. AND PETER! Nowhere in the Bible does it record that Peter asked for a second chance to be right with Jesus. Rather, in John 21:15-19, he asked

Peter three times whether he loved Him. When Peter responded "yes" each time, Jesus commands were "Feed my sheep" and "Follow me."

This does not mean that Peter lost his salvation and got it back later. Galatians 2:11-17 records that Paul also had to rebuke Peter and Barnabas for not wanting to eat with the Gentiles. But he never said, "Peter, you and Barnabas need to pray for your salvation again." There is a big difference between a rebuke and a loss of salvation. You can never lose your salvation in Christ. John 3:16 says that whoever believes in him shall not perish but have everlasting life. It does not say that whoever believes in him will not perish except if you stop believing. Romans 10:9 says that if you confess with your mouth that Jesus is Lord and believe in your heart that God rose him from the dead you will be saved. It does not say that you will be saved only if you continue to believe. That false teaching has hurt a lot of Christian singles because when they fall short of the glory of God, they think that God has left them. God's spirit came and went in the Old Testament. When the spirit of the Lord departed from King Saul, David said in Psalm 51:11, "Cast me not away from thy presence; and take not thy holy spirit from me." But no New Testament Christian should be praying that prayer. Under the New Covenant, Jesus never leaves us, nor forsakes us. We are not alone, even when we feel we are.

Practically speaking, there are many things Christian singles can do to don the full armor of God and combat loneliness. As a Christians single myself, I like to keep life exciting while enjoying the blessings I have in Christ. I like to attend Promise Keepers, which is an all-male Christian group, whose members are men from all walks of life. I also enjoy Christian retreats and singles ministries where I can teach singles from a singles view. And I enjoy watching Christian movies and hanging out with my Christian friends. There's just so much you can do to avoid that so-called state of loneliness.

When I was teaching a singles ministry at my home church in Maryland, we met every Wednesday night and watched a Christian movie. Afterward, we'd discuss the movie and apply it to our lives as singles. All of us would bring food to eat during the movie and afterward. We all just had a great time with the Lord.

Sometimes we'd have a game night where we'd play games that would teach us the Word of God. Another week, we might come together with Christian singles from other churches for fellowship. The week after, we'd go to their church.

You might also try doing a fund raiser for your singles ministry so your group doesn't always have to depend on church funds. I mean, if God has provided the money, great! But the point is to live out our lives as productive singles doing productive works for His kingdom. Hold car washes. Raise money to go on singles trips in the States and overseas. You can even go to Israel as a singles group and walk where our Lord and Savior walked! Or, go to Greece and walk the same routes Paul took on his missionary journeys. You can also go to where the reformer Martin Luther ministered. There are so many activities we can engage in to avoid that so-called loneliness state. God gave us our brains, and we have to use them.

The point is that as Christians, we need to be creative in our walks. Philippians 2:12 urges us to "work out your own salvation with fear and trembling." We need to know in our hearts that we belong to Christ and that we are free. As a result, we should be enjoying our lives as Christians singles. 1 Corinthians 10:31 tells us, "Whether therefore ye eat, or drink, or whatsoever ye do, do all to the glory of God." Please do not miss out on the great life that God has for His people who love Him. 1 Corinthians 2:9 says, "No eye has seen, no ear has heard, no mind has conceived what God has prepared for those who love him." Pray and ask God to guide your footsteps in how to either start or serve in a singles ministry, and for Him to put the right people in your path to help you. God wants us to be fruitful!

Chapter 10

"I'm Tired of Being Single!"

oday we live in a society where everything has to be "RIGHT NOW!" When we turn on our TVs, we normally use the remote control because we can't take the time to get out of our chairs. When we want something to eat, we get fast food because we don't want to take the time to cook at home. And even when we do, we use the microwave to "nuke" our meals in seconds. The list goes on and on. We live in a fast-paced society that seems to be getting faster, and even Christians are getting to be products of that environment, even though we're called to be different from the world. Romans 12:1-2 says:

"I beseech you therefore, brethren, by the mercies of God, that ye present your bodies a living sacrifice, holy, acceptable unto God, which is your reasonable service. And be not conformed to this world: but be ye transformed by the renewing of your mind, that ye may prove what is that good, and acceptable, and perfect, will of God."

1 John 2:15-17 says:

"Love not the world, neither the things that are in the world. If any man love the world, the love of the Father is not in him. For all that is in the world, the lust of the flesh, and the lust of the eyes, and the pride of life, is not of the Father, but is of the world. And the world passeth away, and the lust thereof: but he that doeth the will of God abideth for ever."

In addition, I encourage you to read Jesus' prayer for His disciples in John 17 because He talks about the fact that God the Father gave Jesus the 12 disciples out of the world and how He wants His Father to protect them from the evil one. The fact is, we are in this world to be a lamp to the lost, and in order to be that lamp, we need to be different from the world. James 4:4 says anyone who chooses to be a friend of the world is an enemy of God. The world is against God and everything He stands for.

Sadly enough, many Christian singles today seem to be conforming to the world. They lack the patience in waiting for God to choose a mate for them. As a result, they start dating nonbelievers, they meet people over the internet who are thousands of miles away, and they travel across international borders all because they believe that since God hasn't brought someone to them, that they're supposed to venture out on a wild goose chase and claim that it's God's will. Christian singles want to hurry out and find love just like the world when God has not answered your prayers. Remember, though, you are not like the world and are not to conform to it. Anyone who conforms to the world is an enemy of God.

When we become inpatient, we fall into sin. God already knows your needs even before you ask him because He is all knowing. Matthew 6:7-8 says:

"But when ye pray, use not vain repetitions, as the heathen do: for they think that they shall be heard for their much speaking. Be not ye therefore like unto them: for your Father knoweth what things ye have need of, before ye ask him."

Here, Jesus is telling His disciples two things. First, we're not even supposed to pray like the world does. Yes, folks! Believe it or not, people in the world pray! Proverbs 28:9 says, "If anyone turns a deaf ear to the law, even his prayers are detestable." When Jesus taught His disciples how to pray using what we refer to today as "the Lord's Prayer," in Matthew 6:9-15, notice that He instructed them to pray that the Lord's will be done, not their own. Secondly, He told them that their Father knew what they needed before they even ask Him. Now, that doesn't mean we're not supposed to pray, but the verse speaks about God's omniscience.

God knew that the first man, Adam, needed a helper. Genesis 2 doesn't say that Adam asked God for a wife; rather it simply says in verse 18, "It is not good for the man to be alone. I will make a helper suitable for him." So, even though Adam never asked for a soulmate, God still provided him one. God knows your needs just like He knew Adam's. And quite honestly, no one has an excuse for being alone in the world today, even if we're not married. Adam was the only person on the earth at the time. Today, there are millions upon millions of people here. Nobody is alone in the world today. So, do not grow tired of doing God's will, for that would be sin. 2 Corinthians 4:1 says, "Therefore, since through God's mercy we have this ministry, we do not lose heart." Verses 15-17 of that same chapter continue:

"All this is for your benefit, so that the grace that is reaching more and more people may cause thanksgiving to overflow to the glory of God. Therefore we do not lose heart. Though outwardly we are wasting away, yet inwardly we are being renewed day by day. For our light and momentary troubles are achieving for us an eternal glory that far outweighs them all."

And Hebrews 12:3 says: "Consider him who endured such opposition from sinful men, so that you will not grow weary and lose heart."

Once again, God's will is for us to reach more and more people, according to these verses. And as single people, we have a greater opportunity to do that than we would if we were married, because we don't have the concerns of a spouse. Do not look at what the world is doing because that will burn up in the fire because it is not of God. Matthew 13:40-41 says:

"As the weeds are pulled up and burned in the fire, so it will be at the end of the age. The Son of Man will send out his angels, and they will weed out of his kingdom everything that causes sin and all who do evil."

I know that seeing a happy couple showing affection for one another in a shopping mall looks really appealing, especially if you're struggling with your singleness. You wish you were in their shoes. But how do you know that is a Godly couple you're seeing? And even if you asked them, and they said, "Yes, we're Christians," that doesn't make it true. The point is that as Christians, we should be fulfilled in Christ and not be in want because the Lord Jesus is our Shepherd. Philippians 4:13 says, "I can do everything through him who gives me strength."

Is your strength in the Lord today? Have you asked Him to

give you strength for your daily walk with Him? Don't take your eyes off Jesus, like Peter did, or you will sink. When you stay focused on Christ, you will actually be able to face trials with joy. James 1:2-3 says:

"Consider it pure joy, my brothers, whenever you face trials of many kinds, because you know that the testing of your faith develops perseverance."

In addition, you will not be paying attention to the things of the world, because you will be focusing on your joy in the Lord, developing your faith, and persevering in His work. You will not have time to want things "right now" because when you have really been in the presence of the Lord, you will never want to leave. You will have the peace that passes understanding according to Philippians 4:7.

In being in His presence, I learned patience because I learned that I don't want that kind of peace to ever leave me. As young David writes in Psalm 23, "He maketh me to lie down in green pastures: he leadeth me beside the still waters.." He gives me rest, and He will give you rest too, if you let Him. To get that rest, you really have to know Him and spend time in His presence. You will never grow tired of the will of God because you will be doing Kingdom work. You won't have time to be like the world if you focus on Christ. So, don't be in such a rush to get married. I know what it means to want to be with someone, and at times it seems like singleness is forever even if you don't want it to be. But do not worry about a time line. That's not your concern; it's His. Nothing in this present world can compare to what the Lord has for those who love him and follow his commands. Paul says that the race is not given to the swiftest, but the one who endures to the end.

Will you endure to the end? The choice is yours. God gave us free will to make our own choices. God never wants us to make bad choices. Since He loves freely and not forcefully, He will always give us freedom to make choices. Everyone who has died and gone to heaven did so because it was there choice. Everyone in Hell is there because they chose to be there. Lucifer was one of the most beautiful creatures God ever made and one of God's top angels, and he still chose to go to Hell and other angels chose to go to hell with him. God even gave the angels choices! Those who are

in heaven are there because they choose to be there. And they
know all about bad choices because they were there when the others descended into hell.

Now, the angels don't reproduce like humans because
Matthew 22:30 says they neither marry nor are given to marriage.
But my point is that as Christian singles, we have to be careful to
make choices that are in line with God's will. Make good choices
for the Lord, and He will reward you. Do not try to be the first in
your singles group to arrive at the altar because you will burn out
before the race ends. Keep persevering!

Epilogue

Soul Winning Is the Key

emember, as a child of God, you are free. Remaining single should not be a burden. And when the Lord decides that you're ready to marry, getting married will not be a burden as long as Jesus is the focus of your marriage. When you're single, that's the time to prepare yourself for that spouse, through prayer, fasting, and meditating on the Word of God daily. Just like the apostle Paul wrote in 1 Corinthians 7:27-29:

"Are you married? Do not seek a divorce. Are you unmarried? Do not look for a wife. But if you do marry, you have not sinned; and if a virgin marries, she has not sinned. But those who marry will face many troubles in this life, and I want to spare you this."

In other words, yes, Paul knew that married people face many trials in life, but above all, he wanted the Corinthians to live the best life they could that would glorify God. If you're single and want to stay single, great! If you marry, great! Marriage was created by God and makes Him happy. Marriage is not a sin. Scripture says that if you have found a wife (or a husband) you've found a good thing.

A final word to the ladies: As I have stated in earlier chapters, men have been appointed throughout scripture to be the spiritual leaders in their household; therefore, it's their job to choose their spouses. I do not recommend that women take the initiative in finding a mate and leading the relationship. Why? Because your future mate will never be able to grow into the Godly male headship role that he is supposed to grow into if he is not leading the relationship. So, please continue to grow into a Godly woman, just as he will grow into a Godly man. Pray that God will send you your chosen mate, if that is what you want. But please wait patiently on the Lord, and you will be rewarded with a Godly spiritual leader for your life. One of the greatest honors you can receive from God as women is to let God bring your Godly mate to you. You don't have to break a sweat. Just pray for a spirit-filled man who honors God with his whole being. Neither of you will be perfect creatures, but as Jesus Christ is the head of your lives, He will be the head of your marriage.

And if you decide to remain single for the rest of your life, the Bible says you've done even better. You will continue to be fulfilled in ways that only a single person understands. I am still single myself, and the idea of being single for the rest of my life seems so much more relaxing and less difficult that my life would be if I got married. That doesn't mean I don't have any problems, but I have learned to be content in the current state where I was called. I don't know whether I will remain single for the rest of my life or not, but I absolutely will not live in mental torment hoping that God will bring me a wife. I have learned to enjoy the current moment that God has given me. We're not guaranteed tomorrow. We're not guaranteed 10 minutes from now. That's why we need to live each and every day living the very best life we can possibly live for Christ.

Single people are simply freer to do more work for the Lord, and freer from the cares of this world. Even if I decide that it's God's will for me to marry one day, I can look back and say, "Man, I had a great time in the Lord being single," and not "Man, I was sure in mental torment. I wished I could have been more relaxed." I thank God for every moment of my life. Even now, as I'm writing this book, I'm working for the Lord. If I were in mental torment, I would be useless to God. As you do more and more work for the lord, you'll experience those "desperation, torment" moments less and less. Before you know it you'll feel like you've never been in torment in your life. It's all about focus. When you're busy for the Lord, He gives you the peace that passes all understanding.

Waiting patiently for the Lord also brings God-fearing wisdom. The choices you make as a mature believer will be far better than the choices you would make early in your Christian walk. When you are a babe in Christ, you will make babe choices. When you are seasoned in Christ, you will make seasoned choices. I'd much rather make seasoned choices than babe choices, especially as a seasoned Christian. I've even seen seasoned Christians make babe choices. How is that possible, you may ask? When seasoned Christians lose their patience with God, they make babe choices.

Abraham, the father of many nations, was a seasoned believer who made a babe choice to satisfy the moment in his walk with the Lord when he and his wife Sarah decided to take matters into their own hands, because they didn't believe that he and Sarah would ever have a child together, despite God's promises. So, Sarah told Abraham to sleep with Hagar, and Hagar had a child. It didn't turn out to be beneficial, however. God had already promised that He would deliver His Word, but we just have to believe and wait patiently. Don't create an Ishmael in your life. Genesis 16:12 said that Ishmael would be a wild donkey of a man and live in hostility with all of his brothers.

Have you created any wild donkeys in your single walk with God today? I know I have. You may be a single parent because you had a baby outside of marriage, and the baby's father is nowhere to be found. Maybe he's around somewhere, but he doesn't want to marry you. Where does that leave you and your child? If you're a man, the same thing may have happened to you, and the baby's mother doesn't want to marry you, or won't even let you see your child. So, where does that leave you? My point is that no matter how bad a situation may seem, God is faithful. Just like He kept His promise to Abraham, He will keep His promises to you.

Are you willing to move forward in God's will and not your own? The past is the past. You cannot go back, but with God, you can live life with no regrets. Be wise in the choices you make. Even if your past resurfaces occasionally, God will continue to move your forward and do GREAT things for the one He loves. We all have Ishmaels in our lives somewhere, but there will come a time where there will be no more death, no more sickness, and nor more crying. We will live in pure happiness with the Lord of Hosts. We will be in heaven with God and all the saints that we've read about all our lives in the 66 books of the Bible. We will see them all. You

will see loved ones once again. That is the hope we should be looking to---seeing Jesus in Heaven where we will be with Him for all
eternity.

For the time being, we should be out winning souls for the
kingdom of God so they to may share in this blessed hope.
Proverbs 11:30 says, "The fruit of the righteous is a tree of life; and
he that winneth souls is wise." And Matthew 28:19-20 urges us to
"Go ye therefore, and teach all nations, baptizing them in the name
of the Father, and of the Son, and of the Holy Ghost: Teaching them
to observe all things whatsoever I have commanded you. "

That is our Great Commission as Christians---not just single
Christians, but ALL Christians. If you can win souls without any
distractions, then praise God! If you do have distractions while
you're winning souls, then still praise God! Today, right now, as
Christian singles, are you winning souls for the kingdom of
Heaven? Are you making a difference in someone's life? Are you
being fruitful for the kingdom of God by your works? And when
was the last time you led somebody to Christ?

Brothers and sisters, go and make disciples. For Jesus says in
Matthew 28:20, "and, lo, I am with you always, even unto the end
of the world. Amen."

www.ingramcontent.com/pod-product-compliance
Lightning Source LLC
Chambersburg PA
CBHW032034090426
42741CB00006B/817

9 780615 156798